MW01491493

HOW TO KEEP FROM GOING BROKE WITH A BROKER

A GUIDE TO OPENING, MAINTAINING AND SURVIVING YOUR BROKERAGE ACCOUNT

HOW TO KEEP FROM
GOING BROKE
WITH A BROKER

A GUIDE TO OPENING, MAINTAINING AND SURVIVING YOUR BROKERAGE ACCOUNT

Richard A. Lewins

Bascom Hill Publishing Group
Minneapolis, MN

BASCOM HILL
PUBLISHING GROUP

Bascom Hill Publishing Group
212 3rd Avenue North, Suite 290
Minneapolis, MN 55401
612.455.2293
www.bascomhillpublishing.com

ISBN - 978-1-935098-24-9
ISBN - 1-935098-24-1
LCCN - 2010921779

Cover Design and Typeset by Jenni Wheeler

Printed in the United States of America

To my wife, Naomi, who said,
"You've been talking about this for months; write it already!"

CONTENTS

INTRODUCTION

This book was inspired by my own twelve-plus years of experience in the securities industry as a broker, regional sales manager, regional marketing manager, compliance officer, and in-house counsel for a broker/dealer. I also draw on my legal representation of more than two-hundred clients in securities litigation through arbitration.

My goal is to save you thousands, tens of thousands, or hundreds of thousands of the dollars you have earned, saved, or inherited, and subsequently entrusted to, or are considering entrusting to, a professional to help you manage these funds.

I will describe in detail what you need to know about choosing an investment advisor, the importance of the forms and documents that are the backbone of your account, and what to do to avoid things going bad; and, if they do go bad, what to do then.

Hopefully after reading this book you will be an informed and enlightened consumer of brokerage services. Markets go up and down; there is always a new or improved product to replace the last new and improved product – what remains constant is the basic tenets surrounding the broker/client relationship and what you can and should expect from that relationship. Good luck!

CHAPTER 1
DO I NEED A BROKER?

The answer and the reasons behind the answer to this question have changed over the years.

In order to manage a portfolio effectively you need time, discipline, a plan, and access to information. At one time, even if you had the first two, you probably lacked the rest. That is, you may have had the time to devote to your portfolio and the discipline to make objective, unemotional decisions; however, most people lacked a plan and the access to information.

For an investment plan, most people considered, "buy low, sell high, and don't lose any money" as their plan (That still holds true!). Retirement planning was left to the largesse and/or profitability of employers and the federal government in the form of Social Security.

Investment information once consisted mainly of articles in business publications, reports by rating agencies such as Standard and Poor's or Moody's Investor Services, and research reports and analysis generated by the large brokerage firms. Magazine articles were not timely. Access to Standard and Poor's and Moody's reports required a costly subscription and were not timely. That left the broker.

The broker was the one with access to timely and (hopefully) accurate information on stocks, bonds, mutual funds, and the like. The investing public was lead to believe, rightly or wrongly, that a registered representative/stockbroker/financial advisor/ financial consultant/ financial executive, or whatever label the industry used to describe its sales force, was a trained professional, much like their doctor, lawyer, or accountant. And that this individual had knowledge of and access to all the financial data and information necessary to manage and create wealth and financial security. Without this person to impart this knowledge and acumen, the investor could do little more than throw darts at a board to make financial choices.

Limited access to limited information is no longer a problem. In fact, the pendulum has swung the other way. Investors are bombarded with information from all sides from magazines such as *Forbes, Fortune, Smart Money,* and *Business Week*; papers such as *Barron's,* the *Wall Street Journal*, *Investors Daily*, and *USA Today*; cable stations such as CNBC, MSNBC, and Bloomberg; and the ever-present Internet with instant news and chat rooms. Additionally, there are numerous books to assist you. All combine to effectively overload potential investors with information, or in some cases misinformation, on any given investment strategy, opportunity, or investment vehicle. A lack of information is not the problem, but rather the inability to process and synthesize all the available information into a useful investment plan.

In the past, the broker positioned himself as one of the only sources of knowledge and information. Now, given the sheer magnitude of growing information, the industry positions brokers not necessarily as sources, but instead as managers, distillers, and filterers of that information.

Brokers take on many titles that incorporate the terms, "manager," "advisor," "specialist," and "certified." Their goal is to convince you that you need them to develop an active, long-term investment strategy that will outperform a passive, index-based portfolio (net of expenses), while at the same time doing so with less volatility. They need to convince you that the products and services they recommend are worth the upfront costs and ongoing expenses associated with them. The retail brokers and brokerage firms of the past were much more reliant on the traditional "commission per trade" model.

In recent years they have become much more dependent on ongoing revenue streams from products that charge annual expenses and fees, as well as earning margin interest by convincing you that borrowing against your securities for whatever purposes is suitable. Therefore, their ability to convince you that you "need" them is all the more critical to their profitability.

So, do you need a broker? Like many things in life the answer is, *it depends*. The issues are still much the same as they were years ago: saving for retirement with growth measured against toler-ance and ability to withstand risk and volatility, preserving pur-chasing power, and not outliving our savings. Can you or, maybe more importantly, *do you want to* manage these issues on your own given the plethora of information and resources available to guide you without paying a fee or commission? If the answer is yes, in all likelihood you do not need a broker. If, however, you feel you do not have the desire to arm yourself with the tools and information to manage these issues, and you are willing to pay the price (sometimes exorbitant) to have someone else do it for you, then a financial advisor should probably be in your life or in your future.

CHAPTER 2
TYPES OF BROKERS AND BROKERAGE ACCOUNTS

If you have determined you need or want someone to assist you with investing, then choosing the type of brokerage relationship that makes the most sense for you is your next consideration. Let's examine the choices.

Full Service vs. Discount

A full-service broker is what you can find at a firm such as Merrill Lynch. Brokers at such firms offer a wide range of investment products and services that have a compensation agreement with the firm. The brokers are compensated for selling these products and services and/or gathering assets to be managed by the firm or outside managers. They may also be compensated on the interest their firm receives as a result of your decision to borrow money from them, using your investments as collateral, also known as "going on margin."

These brokers have usually been through some type of training program to prepare for the securities licensing examination, as well as engaging in additional and ongoing sales training on the various products and services their firm offers. Contrary to popular belief, however, there is no prerequisite educational or vocational training to become a broker. Unlike doctors, lawyers, engineers, and other professionals who must successfully complete years of a rigorous academic curriculum before sitting for licensing exams and being allowed to ply their trade, brokers need only pass a multiple choice exam given by the industry's self-regulatory organization, FINRA, and pay a fee to be able to identify themselves as investment professionals. Today's broker could very well have been yesterday's patio furniture salesman. A caution: while the brokerage industry spends millions of dollars in marketing and advertising to position their brokers as professionals, in reality these are just highly paid salespeople who sell financial products and services (instead of patio furniture).

What you are paying for with a full-service broker is active management and advice about the purchase and sale of investments and services. But, be aware that you are also paying for the high overhead that comes with full service; therefore, only those investments and services that generate fees and/or commissions to the broker and his firm are likely to be presented. Put differently, when dealing with a full-service broker, with the possible exception of a money market account, you will not be shown or recommended investments and/or services that do not generate a fee or commission to the broker and his firm!

Besides direct compensation in the form of fees and commissions, brokers at full-service firms may also receive compensation in the form of gifts, trips, dinner, travel, bonuses, recognition, etc., from their firm and/or the companies whose products and services they sell to you.

Sales contests are commonplace in full-service firms. Like any other sales organization, on occasion brokerage firms find themselves with too much inventory in a particular stock or bond, and they need to move it. They will offer their sales force added incentive in the form of higher than normal commissions or payout to move the merchandise (similar to shoe salesmen being offered a bonus for pushing out "pm's" – preferred merchandise).

Most mutual fund companies and insurance companies that sell investments such as variable annuities have wholesalers working for them who have assigned territories, much like a traveling salesman has a territory. Their goal, and their compensation, is based on how much of their funds or annuities they can get a broker to sell. They wine and dine their customers (the brokers) in order to get them to sell their products to you. Again, at a full-service firm you will not be recommended an investment or service that does not generate money to the firm and/or the broker.

With the exception of high commission products such as variable and equity indexed annuities, more and more full-service brokers are moving away from the "commission for transaction" model to the "ongoing fee" model. There are many reasons for this, but one of the main reasons is predictability of income for the broker. With the fee-based model, the broker sells you on the idea of a managed account. You are not charged for transactions, but instead are charged an annual fee, usually paid quarterly, to have your account professionally managed, either by the broker or by an outside manager with whom the brokerage firm has a compensation arrangement.

With this model the broker turns into a money gatherer, knowing that the more money he gathers to manage, the more he will be compensated. And that compensation will come every month, quarter, or year, whether or not there are transactions. His only concern is to convince you that the manager he has selected is doing a good job, or that he can find you a better manager in the event that you are not happy with that manager's results. Again, bear in mind you will not be recommended to a manager that does not have some type of compensation arrangement with the broker's firm.

Discount brokers and brokerage firms, such as Schwab and Fidelity, are for those who feel they do not need that one-to-one relationship with a broker and are comfortable making their own decisions. Most of the licensed brokers at these firms are paid a salary to facilitate the transactions the client wants to execute. They are not in the business of dispensing recommendations, and in most cases are forbidden from doing so by the firms' policies and procedures.

Additionally, your options are not limited to products that have a commission attached to them. In the case of mutual funds, where at a full-service firm you would only be shown those fund families that have a commission or "load," be it on the front end or the back end so the broker can get paid, discount firms have the ability to offer "no load" funds, which pay no commissions. Index funds are funds that track a particular market or market segment and are usually only offered in no-load form; therefore, you will never see those offered by a full-service firm, but instead through discount firms.

For those interested only in execution services from a broker as opposed to advice, discount firms are usually more competitive in their commission or execution fees, as they do not have the overhead of sharing commissions with their brokers and maintaining costly research departments.

Fee-only Financial Planner

While many brokers market themselves as financial planners/advisors/wealth managers, these are for the most part little more than titles meant to impress you and inculcate a sense of a trusted and learned professional rather than a "salesperson." The problem or issue is that at the end of the day whatever they call themselves, their money is made by selling you products and/or services. Rightly or wrongly, their intentions and advice will always be clouded in the fact that they only receive compensation if they sell you something.

There are some individuals who have gone beyond the role of salesperson and, through training and certification, have become financial planners in the truer sense of the word. They may have taken courses in tax, cash flow management, estate law, and retirement planning, which provide them with the background and knowledge to assist in developing a true financial plan that involves more than just finding products to sell to meet objectives. True, they may sell products as an adjunct to their planning business, but there is at least the indication that the products are in accordance with a true plan, which takes into account the total financial picture.

However, outside of the brokerage firms, there is a subset of financial planners that are financial planners in the truest sense of the word, in that they derive their income from the advice and planning they offer. They are known as fee-only financial planners. As the title indicates, they do not sell traditional financial products such as stocks, bonds, mutual funds, or annuities, or earn a fee from placing your assets with a money manager. Instead they offer a product known as a financial plan, for a fee.

You meet with them much like you would with a doctor if you were going in for a physical, health assessment, and plan of care. They will ask you about your assets, lifestyle, cash flow, objectives, time frames for meeting objectives and your tolerance for risk. These are many of the same questions you might be asked by a traditional broker; the difference, however, is the end game. With the broker, the end game is the sale of products or services, while with the fee-only planner the end game is the assessment itself and a plan that comes from that assessment to identify ways to reach your financial objectives and goals. Brokers do not typically charge or charge much for their plan, because as mentioned they get a commission and/or fee on what you buy. Fee-only planners on the other hand may charge handsomely for their time and work product.

Physical health and fiscal health are not static, but dynamic. As with your physical health, where you are advised to receive annual checkups, there will likely be ongoing costs to be paid to the fee-only planner associated with maintaining your fiscal health. This may include periodic reviews and or adjustments to the plan as your life circumstances dictate.

These costs have to be factored into your investment results in the same way you factor in commissions and fees from the products and services you buy from full-service and discount brokers. They are a drag on performance and add to a cost that must be accounted for when figuring your return on your investments.

Index Funds

If you have determined that you do not want or need a broker, but you want to participate in the markets, or have been advised to make investments by a financial planner, index funds may be the way to go.

A market index is a method of measuring a market as a whole. The market can be American stocks, biotech stocks, small-cap stocks, growth stocks, long-term bonds, intermediate term bonds, short-term bonds, or any other market of interest. An index fund is a collective investment scheme that aims to replicate the movements of a group of items of a specific financial market, or a set of rules of ownership that are held constant, regardless of market conditions. These funds typically carry low or no sales loads, and low internal costs and fees to manage. Investing in these is a way to participate in and diversify holdings across a broad spectrum of assets and asset classes.

Because they have no load, and therefore nothing to pay a broker a commission from, your full-service broker will not recommend these investments, regardless of their applicability to your situation. They can be purchased through a discount broker as these brokers do not work on commission, or in some cases they can be purchased directly from the fund company.

CHAPTER 3
HOW DO I CHOOSE A BROKER?

The same way porcupines mate, very carefully. While many things have changed or evolved in the securities industry, how you get a broker has remained relatively unchanged. You get a broker in one of five ways:

1. Referral
2. Response to a Cold Call
3. Attend a Seminar
4. Walk in; Place a Cold Call Yourself
5. Affinity Group

Referral

This is the most common method and has been for many years. You have come into a lump sum of money, or you want to start a systematic investment plan, or someone told you about a "can't miss" stock, and you don't have a broker. What to do. Well, you may not know a broker but chances are you know someone who does. A family member, a close friend or a co-worker; even a stranger you meet in a social setting who can't help talking about how great his investments are doing. The point is someone you know or meet will have, or know, a broker and will be happy to give you his or her name and number, and most people feel more comfortable with this "stamp of approval."

When dealing with an unfamiliar situation or experience most of us look for company as opposed to charting a new course ourselves. Obtaining a referral satisfies that need. Even though it is your money (and your objectives and risk tolerance may be completely different from the person giving you the name and number of a broker), you can take comfort in the fact that you are not alone. Someone else you know is dealing with this person.

The reality is, in most cases, you have no idea what, if any, due diligence this person did in selecting the broker now referred to you. Maybe it was a referral in the first place. Maybe it is a friend or relative that the person feels compelled to do business with. Maybe the broker was found through one of the other four methods listed above. The point is, you need to do a little digging and due diligence yourself.

Is the person giving the referral similar to you? What this means is: does this person have similar investment objectives and tolerance for risk as you? Is the person in a similar place in life as you? Is the person trying to accumulate wealth or preserve it? Is the person more interested in growth or income? Does the person take an active role in his/her investments or does he/she sit back and let the broker run things?

These are important questions because even though in theory a broker can be all things to all people, in reality, most brokers have a certain investment philosophy and mindset and tend to cultivate clients with similar philosophies and mindsets. This is not a hard and fast rule, but many claimants' attorneys have noticed that brokers with an aggressive mindset do not do well with or for clients that do not share that mindset, and that troubles arise when a conservative client is recommended to a broker who does not share that affinity for low risk.

Responding to a Cold Call

Cold calling, or "smiling and dialing" as it was referred to in the old days, is still a key weapon in a broker's arsenal. Simply put, it is getting an unsolicited call from a broker seeking your business. The math on this method of acquiring clients goes something like this: Make one-hundred calls to people you don't know and who don't know you. Ten will agree to meet with you or allow you to contact them further, and one or two will become clients. Do this everyday for a year or two and you will be set as a broker.

Brokers that use this method don't usually just pick up the phone book and start in the "A's." They buy lists that target people by zip-code, income, employment, hobbies, etc. – anything that can provide an insight into your potential investment proclivities.

The skilled cold callers do not try to sell you on the first call; they just want to whet your appetite and gauge your interest in investing. They do not care if you hang up; in fact they prefer that to keeping them on the phone if you are not potentially interested. Remember: to them, it is a numbers game. Each hang-up gets them closer to someone who will say yes.

At one time, Dunn & Bradstreet was a company that collected data on businesses and individuals. Cards that had an individual's income, net worth, and occupation, etc., were sold to brokerage firms who then passed them out to their brokers as leads. By making one-hundred dials a day, a broker thought he had a ticket to financial freedom and fortune.

The thing to understand and remember if and when you are cold-called by a broker: at that point in time you are just a number, a means to an end for the broker. He is almost as happy to have you reject his call as to accept it.

Understand that the more time you spend on the phone with a broker, the more likely you are to succumb to his pitch. This is especially true of the elderly and/or lonely. Brokers are professional salespeople. They are educated and trained on how to make you feel comfortable and how to overcome your objections. Tell them you have no money; they will have a comeback. Tell them this is not a good time to talk; they will get you to commit to a time later. They will have a comeback for any excuse. If you do not want to choose your broker via an anonymous voice on the phone, then politely but firmly say, "No, thank you," and hang up.

Attend a Seminar

More and more brokers are using seminars as a way to find new clients. For brokers that do not have a fear of public speaking this can be a very effective way of presenting their pitch to large groups of people. The invitation is almost always couched in terms of giving you information or education, but at the end of the day the brokers who put on these seminars are there to sell you a product or an investment plan of some sort, something that will generate a commission or fee for them.

Ads are run in the local paper or mailers are sent a week or two before the date of the seminar, asking for people to call the office to make a reservation. The seminar is held at a hotel, with or after dinner. They usually last for forty-five minutes to an hour-and-a-half, during which time the broker will go over the features and benefits of the product or service he is selling. The broker's goal is to convince you to set up a one-on-one meeting in their office/your home. They rarely close a sale at the seminar. They are looking for long-term clients, not one-hit sales.

Many clients met their broker at a seminar, especially if they are retirees. The fact pattern is eerily similar: They have little or no investment experience. Their only investments are in their retirement account through work. They saved diligently, contributing the maximum allowed to their plan, and their plan allowed for the purchase of company stock, which is where they put the majority of their money. If there were choices to be made regarding investments and allocation among those choices, they usually consulted with their supervisors or superiors at work, as opposed to an investment professional.

When the opportunity presented itself to access the funds, (which depending upon how much they earned in salary, how much they contributed, whether it was matched by the company, how it was invested and for how long), the amount could be upwards of a million dollars, or more.

Now they are faced with a life-altering situation. Either through involuntary layoff, voluntary lay off, or for age/health-related circumstances, they need their retirement savings to be their source of income.

Most of these folks never earned more than fifty thousand dollars a year and are not looking to increase their standard of living, just maintain it, if possible. They do not have any concept of modern portfolio theory, or non-correlating assets, or risk/return analysis, or what is a reasonable distribution rate. They are looking for someone more knowledgeable than they to guide and advise them.

Some were offered, through their plans or employers, some type of lifetime annuity that will pay monthly until they die, and that sounded good. But then they hear about or are invited to a seminar especially for them. This seminar is being put on at a nice hotel or restaurant where a nice meal will be served. The seminar is being hosted by John/Jane Smith, a wealth manager/vice president/certified retirement specialist, etc., with Dewey, Cheatem & Howe brokerage firm.

You feel comfortable going to the seminar because after all it being given especially for you and your fellow co-workers. It may have been advertised on the breakroom wall, or you received a handwritten invitation. There is no cost or obligation, and you are assured that no one will try to sell you anything. The people giving the seminar are INVESTMENT PROFESSIONALS, or at least that is what all the firm's advertising and all the fancy titles and initials after their names would have you believe.

I have yet to have a client tell me that they did not perceive their broker in the same light as they viewed doctors, lawyers, and accountants. They perceive brokers to be people with special knowledge and special training, and that is precisely how the firms want you to perceive them. These firms spend millions and millions of dollars in advertising and promotion to convince you that they are investment professionals, that they know more than you, and that you can trust them to take care of you and your money.

The story my clients are told at the seminar is basically this: we can do better for you than the annuity you were offered through work. If you give us your money to manage, we will see to it that you can have at or near the same level of income in retirement as you had while working, while at the same time maintaining or even growing the principal.

The clients are shown graphs and charts of historical returns in the stock market for the last seventy years. They are told that over long periods of time the stock market has always outperformed other types of investments, and that on average the market will return between nine and eleven percent per year. They are told that an individual plan will be worked up tailored specifically to their investment objectives, needs, and goals by investment professionals with the knowledge and resources to protect and grow the client's savings.

This chapter is about choosing a broker rather than the suitability of recommendations you may receive. As a method of deciding on whom to invest your money with, attending a seminar is only a step, and a small one at that, above responding to a cold call. As with a cold call, a seminar is a numbers game for the broker and a shot in the dark for you. You may feel comfortable that you are surrounded by people like you, and that you are in a nice place, possibly being fed a nice meal, but none of those are good reasons to choose this person to entrust your life savings.

Walk in; Place a Cold Call Yourself

At most large offices of large brokerage firms there is a "broker of the day." His or her job is to field all in-person and phone inquiries that come from people who do not have accounts already.

What can make this method effective is that it incorporates an essential element in choosing a broker: compatibility. Compatibility means similar or equal investment philosophies. You want someone who can understand, empathize, and/or relate to your investment objectives, needs, and tolerance for risk. One of the best ways to determine this is to meet the broker face to face and/or ask specific questions over the phone.

Remember, this is a buy/sell arrangement; the broker is the seller and you are the buyer. Just like any other major, important purchase you consider, you need to ask hard, pointed questions that focus on your wants, needs, and concerns. If you don't understand the answers, or feel like you are being talked down to or around, then find another salesperson.

While investing may seem like rocket science, or at least that is what the financial industry would like you to believe; it is not. The more complex and difficult to understand your broker makes it, the less likely the broker or the recommended investment is for you.

Affinity Group

There is a growing trend in affinity group marketing in the area of financial services. Affinity groups are groups of people brought together by a shared experience or background. A member of the group uses that common background or experience as a way to market products and/or services to other members of the group.

Relating it to the topic at hand, there are a significant number of brokers that find their clients based on a shared experience or background that has little or nothing to do with their experience or acumen as a financial advisor. For example, an airline pilot that retires from active duty, becomes securities licensed and registered, and then promotes himself to his former airline pilot friends and associates. He relies on their common background as pilots as a basis for their trust and willingness to do business with him. He hopes that they will equate his skills and acumen as a pilot to his ability to manage money.

There is of course very little correlation to flying a plane with managing money. While you may argue that both require a certain degree of intelligence, and may share certain traits like patience and being cool under pressure, there is no tangible basis for believing that just because a person is a good pilot they will be a good broker. This is not to say that a pilot cannot be a good broker; it is just as a potential client you need to make sure that you make your selection of a financial advisor based on criteria associated with money management and not some unrelated occupation.

Another affinity group where the lines between common interest/ experience and money management can be easily blurred involves the clergy. Specifically, there are a number of spiritual leaders that supplement their non-secular income from other occupations. Some become licensed securities and/or insurance salespersons.

As with the pilot-turned-financial-advisor discussed above, there is no direct correlation between the skills and acumen associated with being an effective spiritual leader and being an effective financial advisor. However, unlike with the pilot, there is an added element to this relationship beyond shared and/or common experience – the spiritual leader/follower relationship. While there are limits, and rightly so, on how much you can trust your financial advisor, the degree of trust and confidence you place in your spiritual advisor is for all intent and purpose limitless. Most people, whether consciously or subconsciously, cannot bring themselves to question any advice their priest, minister, rabbi, etc., may provide. This is a potentially perilous situation when that advice is financial in nature.

You have to feel free and unencumbered to question your broker about what is going on with your account, not fearful or guilty about the repercussions of questioning someone you believe holds the key to your spiritual well-being and salvation. There are enough inherent conflicts of interest in the customer/broker relationship; to add religion, faith, and a sense of dominion to the equation is too precarious.

Some faiths do not allow their leaders to mix secular and non-secular activities within their congregation, but that is the exception not the rule. Therefore it is incumbent upon you to recognize the pitfalls associated with this type of relationship and not let yourself be caught up in the fantasy that by virtue of ordination your money and your spirituality are intertwined with the same person. As with the pilot scenario above, it does not mean that a spiritual leader cannot also be a good broker; but the potential risks and conflicts associated with doing business with *your* spiritual leader will most likely far outweigh any possible benefit.

Other Considerations

There are three other things you want to consider when choosing a broker: history of complaints, large firm vs. small firm, and support staff.

History of Complaints

Simply put, has anyone ever complained about your broker? Anytime a client files a written complaint against the broker, either with the broker or his supervisor, the complaint is supposed to be part of the broker's permanent record. That record is kept on the broker's CRD (Central Registration Depository) with the broker regulatory authority known as FINRA (Financial Industry Regulatory Authority). You can go to the website, www.finra.org, and enter the broker's name to access his CRD. For various reasons, FINRA's information is sometimes not as accurate or up to date as it should be. That is why you should also contact your state's securities commission. They also will have a CRD on any broker licensed and registered to do business in your state, and in my experience it is more reliable and up to date than FINRA.

Ask the broker directly if any customers have complained about him or her! This is a direct question that you want a direct answer to; not some indirect answer like, "Check my CRD; I have no complaints listed." For reasons too technical to go into here, some complaints never get listed or, worse yet, are removed from the CRD. Therefore, a simple direct question to which you want a "yes" or "no" answer is needed. You also want to memorialize this question and answer in writing at the time it is asked and answered. This may be important later if a problem arises.

Just because a broker has had a complaint should not automatically disqualify him in your mind. After all, even the best of us has had unhappy/unreasonable clients who by nature are complainers, especially if you have been in business a long time. If there is a complaint on the CRD or the broker answers your question in the affirmative, ask questions. But in many cases, where there is smoke, there is fire; so a complaint record or history should be taken seriously.

Large Firm vs. Small Firm

Before the proliferation of available research and information on the Internet and in the media, this might have been a bigger issue; but it still remains a consideration nonetheless. Aside from the belief that a smaller firm equates to more personalized attention, you want to know if there is a problem down the road, there will be money available to pay your claim.

You may be surprised to learn that most if not all of the household names in this industry do not carry insurance to cover claims by clients; they simply pay them themselves. It is of the smaller firms that you must be wary. If you want to do business with a smaller firm, ask your broker up front if they have insurance to cover any claims that may be brought against them. Many cases have been turned down because even if the case was won there was no money to collect! Clients are not in need of moral victories, they need real money to compensate them for real harm done to them. Again, get this information in writing.

Support Staff

The availability and quality of support staff is an overlooked but important part of choosing a broker. Most of the more successful brokers, not to be confused with competent brokers, have one or more support people to assist them. Some of these support people are registered, and therefore can take orders. Many are a conduit between you and the broker and, like in most sales organizations, they are the front line in the relationship. If they do not appear to be competent and helpful at the outset then that should be an indicator as to what you can expect from the relationship with the broker.

In some respects choosing a broker is like choosing a significant other; there needs to be trust, understanding, and a commonality of goals and philosophy; however, always remember that at the end of the day the broker is a salesman and you are a customer. He is in the business of selling you financial services and products and, whether it is by a commission or a fee or a combination/hybrid of the two, he and his firm will only show you investments where they make money.

CHAPTER 4
WHAT SHOULD I EXPECT FROM MY BROKER?

Full Disclosure

Let me sum this up in a few words and expand further: expect full disclosure of material facts relating to the investment/strategy recommended, and only suitable recommendations should be accepted.

The formation of the Securities and Exchange Commission and the Securities Act of 1933, and the Securities Exchange Act of 1934 were all predicated on the need for full disclosure in the area of the securities markets. Prior to their formation and passage, investing in securities could best be summed up by the phrase, *caveat emptor*, "Let the buyer beware." As a result, virtually all investments need to be either registered, which requires disclosure through a registration document filed with the Securities and Exchange Commission and/or a prospectus or, if exempt from registration, then disclosure is required through a private placement memorandum/offering circular.

In either case these are usually bland, cumbersome, lengthy, and technical documents, filled with legalese and arcane terminology. Precisely because of this, most people have brokers to tell them what they need to know about what they are being asked to invest in. Most people do not have the time or expertise to read and/or understand these documents. People rely on their brokers to give them all the pertinent and relevant facts, good or bad, about what they are recommending and why they are recommending it. That is what you are paying for, one way or another. The truth, the whole truth, and nothing but the truth about what you are being sold should be expected.

Suitable Recommendations

The other thing you are relying on and should expect from your broker is that they only make recommendations that are right for you. The industry has rules for this as well. The rules are commonly known as the "know your customer" rule, and the "suitability" rule. The essence of both is that before your broker makes a recommendation for you to buy something, sell something, or in some cases, hold on to something you already own, he has to have a reasonable basis for making the recommendation.

Where does that basis come from? It comes from asking you questions about yourself, many of which are part of the account opening process. At a minimum he should ask you the following:

1. Your full legal name

2. Physical address

3. Birth date

4. Employment status

5. Income (if retired, how are you currently meeting your financial needs, i.e. Social Security, pension plan, investment income, other)

6. Tax bracket

7. Net worth (all assets minus all liabilities)

8. Liquid net worth (what of your net worth you can readily convert to cash)

9. Investment experience (hint: if your great aunt Bessie gave you one-hundred shares of stock many years ago, or your neighbor talked you into buying fifty shares of some company his son worked for many years ago, you do not have those years of investment experience. Do not let anyone tell you otherwise.)

10. Investment objective(s) – what are your needs/objectives for these particular monies. (To be discussed in more detail below)

11. Risk tolerance – again, for this particular account and/or sum of money. (To be discussed in more detail below.)

12. Time horizon – when you will need access to this money. Ties into investment risk and objective.

Most of these questions are part of the account opening procedure and documentation, which is covered in more detail in the next chapter, and some of these questions require in-depth analysis in order for the broker to truly know the customer.

For example, a broker's understanding of your investment objective(s) is crucial in determining what type of investment recommendation is suitable for you. If your objective is to have income without risking your capital, then that will define and limit the types of investments that fit that objective. If your objective is to invest for growth, without the need for current income or capital preservation, that will define and open up the types of investments that are suitable to recommend.

Understanding and defining your risk parameters is equally as important as defining your objectives. Most brokers and brokerage firms try to put risk in a box labeled: no risk/conservative/moderate risk, high risk/speculative. But risk is a relative term that is very subjective and personal. Your broker needs to elicit what risk means to you. For your broker, conservative risk may mean that you are willing to lose fifteen to twenty percent of your investment in any give time period, whereas conservative risk may mean to you that you are willing to risk losing five to ten percent of your investment. It is important for you and your broker to be on the same page when it comes to understanding your risk tolerance.

Tell You What You Need to Know, Not What You Want to Hear

You should also expect your broker to tell you when your investment objective and risk tolerance is incongruous or not achievable. For example, some clients say they want to grow their money but not take any risk or lose any principal. Or that they wanted a better return than the bank was offering on CDs but that they couldn't afford to lose anything because they were going to need this money in six months to a year for college tuition or a down payment on a house.

These objectives are mutually exclusive and therefore not achievable. You cannot grow your capital without exposing it to risk of loss. You cannot get a better return than the bank is offering on CDs without exposing your principal to fluctuation that comes with longer-term debt instruments like bonds. It is the responsibility of the broker to tell you if what you want is possible and/or the risks associated with what you want to achieve.

Many clients are sold on an unrealistic and largely unachievable investment strategy that calls for stock market returns/capital gains to replace and provide steady income in retirement. The scenario goes like this: Client is retired or considering retirement. Client would like to maintain the same level of income he/she had when working, or would like to achieve a certain level of income based on what he/she feels is reasonable/necessary to maintain his standard of living, without exposing retirement savings, which are not replaceable. In either case the client's objective amounts to needing a return/distribution rate somewhere between six and ten percent of their retirement savings.

Most of the people are told, not only is that distribution rate achievable, but it can be achieved while growing their retirement savings at the same time. At best/worst they are just told, "Yes, we can do that for you," without any further qualifiers. What they are told, and usually shown in the form of a hypothetical that involve charts and graphs, is that historically the stock market has *averaged* an annual total return of between nine and eleven percent. Therefore as long as they do not withdraw more than nine percent per year, the market will not only meet their income needs but provide them with some growth as well.

What they are not told is that a distribution rate of anything over four to four-and-a-half percent is considered risky and, based on historical data, unsustainable for the twenty to thirty-plus years necessary to fund a typical retirement. What they are not told is what an average return is. That is, it is determined by taking the total returns over a number of years and dividing that number by the number of years to come up with an average. For example, if the market went up one-hundred percent over a ten-year period, the average annual return would be ten percent (100 divided by 10). However, an average may include extended periods of below-average or negative returns that must be considered.

What the charts and graphs in the hypothetical shown to the client usually depict is this average return in a straight line as if it were a constant and consistent rate of return. They do not show the client what is reality – that the market goes up and down to reach the average. While some may think that everyone knows the market goes up and down, what is not shown in the hypothetical is the effect this up and down movement has on the investment strategy.

For example, say you had five-hundred-thousand dollars in your retirement account and, based on your broker's assurances that it would be all right, you were planning on withdrawing seven percent or thirty-five-thousand dollars per year from your account for the next twenty years. You were then shown a hypothetical where the market was depicted as growing ten percent per year in a straight line for twenty years. It would appear that at the end of twenty years that all your income needs would have been met and your account value would have grown from the difference between what you withdrew and the returns from the market.

Now let's say you were shown a different hypothetical, one in which the market was flat for ten years, followed by ten years of twenty percent growth, for the an average return of ten percent per year for twenty years. The average is the same but your account performance is not.

In that first flat year you will pull out seven percent or thirty-five thousand, but now it is seven percent of your principal because there were no returns to provide it to you and you are down to four-hundred-sixty-five thousand dollars. The next year you are pulling out another thirty-five thousand dollars, but again there are no returns to provide this so now you only have four-hundred-thirty thousand dollars of principal left. By the end of the tenth year your principal is down to one-hundred-fifty thousand dollars.

Now the twenty percent growth years start. However in your case that twenty percent growth will not be on the five-hundred thousand dollars you started with but the one-hundred-fifty thousand dollars you are left with. So in that first year of twenty percent growth instead of the twenty percent representing one-hundred thousand dollars to you, it is only thirty thousand dollars. And don't forget you still need to withdraw thirty-five thousand dollars to live on, so effectively your account will show a net negative return in a year that the market was up twenty percent.

Following this formula out for the next nine years: twenty percent growth of the principal left each year minus the thirty-five thousand dollars you need to withdraw each year to live on, will leave you (after twenty years of average ten percent year-over-year growth in the market) with a total of twenty thousand two hundred dollars left in your account from the original five-hundred thousand dollars you started with!

Is this an extreme example? Yes. Can it happen? Yes. What is important about this example is it shows what down or flat years can do to an account's value when you factor in systematic withdrawals. The market does not move in a straight line, but your withdrawals will.

What you want is a broker who will tell you what you need to know to make an informed decision, not what you want to hear for the broker to get the account/sale.

In every case where the distribution rate you are going to receive is in the six to ten percent range you must ask, "What did the broker tell me about this?" Did they say, "It was doable." Or did they say, "Here are your choices; I can give you a four to five percent return with little to no risk to principal, or we can try for a higher return, but take more risk and subject your principal to risk and loss. Which do you prefer?"

Most of my clients were never offered that choice or had it explained in that way. To a person, each would say that given that choice they would have opted for lower returns and less risk, even if that meant lowering their standard of living or taking on a part-time job to supplement the lower returns, because safety of principal was the most important thing to them. They knew that they were not in a position to replace losses to their principal – a fact their broker should know as well.

You want a broker that will tell you what you need to know, not what you want to hear! If you want a cheerleader, go to a high school football game. If you want someone to tell you, "You can do it!" go listen to a motivational speaker. Just because you want a ten percent return on your money with little to no risk does not mean you can have it, or that it is even possible. You want a broker that will be straight with you on what is possible and the risks and costs associated with what you want.

Most people believe that their broker has or should have a duty or an obligation to put clients' needs first before personal needs or those of the firm (otherwise known as a fiduciary duty). This is not a law review article or legal treatise on fiduciary duty, but suffice it to say that this is not the overwhelming or majority opinion based on current case law or statutory law. Unless the broker has control in the form of written discretionary authority/power of attorney or there is some relationship other than just broker/customer, there is some authority that says the broker will not be held to a fiduciary standard; that is, putting your interest above his/hers. A branch manager at one of the brokerage firms once said, "There are three parties to every transaction:

you, your customer, and the firm; two out of the three need to make money on every trade."

That means whenever your broker makes a recommendation to buy or sell a product or service you need to ask yourself and the broker, "How does this fit in with my objective and risk tolerance? What is the benefit to me of what you are recommending? What is the benefit to you?" If your broker cannot or will not answer those questions, it is time to find a new broker.

Let's talk further about suitable recommendations. Brokers are required, and you have every right to expect your broker to make suitable recommendations. Suitable, however, does not necessarily mean profitable. As we discussed above, suitable means appropriate given what your broker knows or should know about you, your objectives, and your tolerance for risk.

For example, if you are gainfully employed or otherwise secure in meeting your day-to-day financial obligations, you're relatively young and/or still in the accumulation of wealth stage in your life, and your needs are not short term, then it would probably be suitable for your broker to recommend growth types of investments, like common stocks. The fact that these stocks may drop in value does not make them unsuitable. The suitability determination is made at the time the investment was recommended, not later when you see if you made or lost money.

Additionally, the suitability determination does not include clairvoyance, i.e., knowing which direction the market is going to go and when. Many potential clients come to a new broker with substantial losses to their portfolios; and when asked what they think the old broker did wrong they answer, "He should have known the market was going to go down and gotten me out." If brokers knew that, they wouldn't be brokers; they would be island owners.

The issue with regard to suitability as it relates to the stock market is not in knowing whether the market will go up or down, but whether it is suitable for you to be in the market in first place and, if so, to what degree.

This concept is commonly referred to as asset allocation, or how much of your money belongs where. There are two schools of thought with regard to asset allocation: (1) Don't put all your eggs in one basket, or (2) put all your eggs in one basket, but watch that basket like a hawk. Very few people have the time or know-how necessary to make the latter work, so most of the world follows the former.

What that translates to in investment terms is that your money should be spread out amongst different types of assets classes and different assets within those classes, so that no one asset or asset class can drag down your entire portfolio. Ideally, what you want is a mix of assets that respond in opposition to each other. These are called non-correlating assets. So when events and circumstances that make one asset class you own respond negatively, they should have the opposite effect on another asset class you own. In that way, you should never experience too many highs or lows, but more of an even keel. That is what most of us want and need. You should expect your broker to assist you in devising an investment plan or strategy where your fortunes do not rise and fall precipitously, but maintains a balance, so that no one event can wreck havoc on your savings.

A perfect example of this was the "tech wreck" of 2000-02. During that time the NASDAQ and the S&P 500 indexes, which were heavily weighted in technology and telecommunications stocks, dropped by over fifty percent. Newspapers, magazines, and television were all talking about how the market downturn wiped out millions of investors. In reality, the stock market as a whole did not suffer all that badly; it was only the technology and telecommunications sectors that were ravaged. If you were invested in a balanced portfolio of stocks along many asset classes or, better yet, in a portfolio balanced between stocks and bonds, which as a general rule act inversely or more in opposite directions, your portfolio would have come close to breaking even or in some cases experienced growth during that time period.

Independent, Unbiased Research

The other lesson we learned from the tech wreck relates to research. The public learned what the industry knew for a long time, that there was an "incestuous" relationship between investment banking and research. Investment bankers are the people at firms that put deals with companies together and, thus, are profit centers. The research department is made up of the people charged with reviewing those companies and offering opinions as to whether you should buy, sell, or hold them, and are cost centers. We came to learn that in many cases the people in research were "motivated" to offer positive opinions and reports on companies that investment banking did deals with or wanted to do deals with, regardless of what they really thought about the company, so that the investment banking people could generate more profit to pay the salaries of the research people.

As a result, you want to make sure your broker is providing you with independent research on investments he is recommending that you buy, sell, or hold on to from people that do not have a stake in whether the investment does well or does poorly.

Communication

You also want a broker who is willing to communicate with you in writing. In a great majority of cases, where a misrepresentation and/or omission of a material fact(s) is the issue, too often it boils down to, "he said/she said." The finder of fact is left trying to come up with a decision based on factors that may have nothing to do with the actual facts; because the facts in dispute are only in the minds and memories of the people telling them, as opposed to having been memorialized at the time in writing.

While phone calls are nice and more personal, this is not dating; it's business. And in business you want things in writing. It is a real red flag when you send your broker an email asking a question or raising an issue about your account and the broker responds back with a phone call to address the issue you raised. This is an indicator that the broker does not want what is said done so in a form that is documented for possible future reference.

At the end of the day, brokers (be they certified this, or registered that, or vice president of the other thing) are salespeople. They make money convincing you to buy what they are selling. But the stakes are much higher because what they are selling can greatly impact your financial health and well-being. You can fix a busted lawnmower; it is harder to fix a busted retirement account. Therefore, you should expect more and need to demand more of this salesperson. You should demand and expect full disclosure, fair dealing and accessibility. You are not a "one size fits all" item, and you should not be treated as such. You should have an investment plan and receive investment service that is uniquely and specifically tailored to you, your objectives, and your risk tolerance.

It may take several meetings with several different brokers to find one that fits, but you wouldn't buy a pair of pants with one leg longer than the other, so why would you accept an ill-fitting broker? If you don't trust your own judgment, seek the advice of someone whose judgment you do trust. But make sure this person is someone that can relate to your individual circumstances. Aside from choosing a spouse, this may be the most important relationship choice you make.

CHAPTER 5
THE IMPORTANCE OF DOCUMENTS AND DOCUMENTS OF IMPORTANCE

As discussed briefly in the last chapter, if things go wrong you do not want to rely on, "he said/she said" evidence, but rather contemporaneous written memorials of key facts. Additionally, the forms and documents that are part and parcel of opening and maintaining a brokerage account form the cornerstone of the regulatory and compliance structure that brokers and brokerage firms are bound by.

New Account Form

The New Account Form (NAF) is the form that contains much of the information discussed previously that your broker should know in order to satisfy the, "know your customer" and/or "suitability" rules. At a minimum this form should contain your full name, address, contact information, employment status, annual income, tax bracket, investment experience, net worth, investment objectives, and risk tolerance.

Your obligation is to give clear, accurate responses to these questions. This is not the time to fudge or allow yourself to be coerced into giving inaccurate information. It is also your obligation to ask questions if you do not understand what is being asked of you. That is especially important with regard to the questions on investment objective and risk tolerance.

Most NAFs have a "check the box" or "rank in order" format for answering these questions. For example, with investment objective your choices may be:

1. Safety

2. Income

3. Growth

4. Speculation

With risk tolerance your choices may be:

1. Conservative

2. Moderate

3. Aggressive

Sometimes there is a descriptive telling you how the brokerage firm interprets those choices, but more often you have no guidance and are either left to your own devices or with asking the broker what they mean.

The most important interpretation, however, is yours! You have the best understanding of what your objective is and you know how much risk you feel comfortable taking. If the choices come with explanations and none of them adequately describe your circumstances, or there are no explanations, you need to write down what you want, regardless of whether or not it fits in the box.

For example if your primary objective is income, but you are not willing to risk losing principal, that is what you need to put on the form. If the form does not have room for comments, you need to make sure comments are appended to or attached to the form. This is critical for two reasons.

This form is what the broker's manager and/or compliance officer looks at when reviewing transactions to see if the transaction is in line with what is written down for investment objectives and risk tolerance. The more accurately you describe your objectives and tolerance, the better job they can do in seeing that your account is being handled properly.

Secondly, if there are problems later on one of the first places the trier of fact will look to attempt to ascertain who is telling the truth with regard to suitability of a particular investment or strategy is the NAF. An accurately and thoroughly filled out NAF should eliminate much of the "he said/she said" debate.

Which leads to the next important point regarding the NAF and all the forms discussed here...who fills them out?

In the overwhelming majority of cases clients say that either the form was filled out by someone other than them, usually the broker or his assistant, or that they are asked to sign the form in blank with the assurance that the broker will fill it in later. *The latter is never acceptable.* The former is more the norm; but you should never sign the form or leave the office until you have had an opportunity to read, understand, and accept what is written about you, particularly your objectives and risk tolerance. If the form is incorrect or not clear to you, make it right.

If you cannot make it clear on the form, then follow up with an email/correspondence where you spell out exactly what you want. Make sure you get written confirmation.

Do not let the broker or his assistant tell you that it doesn't matter what is on the form because they "understand what you want." That may be true, but it doesn't help the people who are charged with reviewing the document for correctness and your trades for suitability. It also will not help the trier of fact years from that day in determining who is telling the truth. The rule of thumb is when there are differing views of who said what to whom, the document will be the tie breaker. You want that tie broken in your favor; and the best way to ensure that is to make sure the document is filled out completely, accurately and thoroughly. What is on that form *does* matter.

Making sure the form is filled out correctly does not mean that you have to be an expert in or have an understanding of securities. You just need to be able to articulate what you want and how much risk you are willing to take to get what you want.

If the form simply does not lend itself to being filled out in such a manner, either because of the choices offered/not offered on the form and/or there is no space to write in what you want, then you must follow up in writing with the broker and request a confirmation from him in writing. This can either be done in the office at the time the NAF is filled in, or in a follow-up email or letter.

The key is written confirmation back from the broker. *Do not sign anything that is not completely and properly filled out.* If a separate writing apart from the NAF is necessary to convey your objective and risk tolerance, indicate so on the form with a "see attached" or "see follow-up letter/email."

Again, this is not only for your benefit but for the benefit of those reviewing the form and subsequent activity in the account. The more of a paper trail you can leave, the less is left to memory or difference of opinion.

Account Verification Form

It is the policy at some brokerage firms that customers not sign the NAF, but instead the customer will be sent a "Verification Form" along with a letter. The letter will ask you to review the enclosed form, which will be an abridged version of the NAF, and to return it if there are any corrections necessary. The letter says that if they do not hear back from you they will assume that everything is correct.

There are several problems with this. Problem one, it assumes that you received it, opened it, read it, and understood what was being asked of you, which is rarely the case. Problem two, it assumes that you understood the consequences of not correcting any errors. Problem three, it assumes that your broker has not instructed you to ignore it, either before you received it after you received it, and you called him to ask him what you should do with it. In almost every case some combination of problems one, two, or three has been an element, particularly number three.

Brokerage firms are subject to an inordinate number of rules and regulations, and most of what they send you in the mail is a product of some rule or regulation. They may send you things that you do not understand, but they will not send you something you should ignore. More on this later in the book in the chapter that discusses things your broker says that get him in trouble.

Questionnaires

Sometimes you are asked to fill out a questionnaire, particularly when a firm is attempting to determine your risk tolerance. This may seem like a thorough and analytical approach to measuring and assessing risk, but all is not as it seems.

Remember, as a general rule brokers are in the business of selling you products, and as a general rule the more risk associated with the product the more the fee/commission. So low-risk products like CDs, money markets, Treasury securities, and AAA-rated bonds have the lowest fees and commissions, whereas higher-risk products such as stocks, stock mutual funds, private placements, and variable annuities have the highest fees and commissions.

Therefore most of these questionnaires, which are designed for the industry's benefit not yours, are designed to determine your risk tolerance to allow for the higher fee and commission generating products. They do this by either weighting the questions or weighting the answers in such a way that your score will put you into a category that allows for risk or riskier investments. *Do not let the tail wag the dog.* If you know that you do not want risk, do not let some questionnaire tell you otherwise.

Margin and Option Agreements

The other common documents you may be asked to sign are margin agreements and option agreements. As a general rule both of these, margin and options, are strategies that are for sophisticated investors and can involve a high degree of risk (covered call writing or hedging are exceptions to this, but we deal here with the most common uses).

Some brokers have been known to hand clients a stack of documents and just tell them to, "sign at the 'X,'" with the idea that they want all the documents signed at once that they may possibly need your authorization on at some future point in time.

Margin involves borrowing money, and in a worse case scenario you could wind up owing more than you have in your account. Options can involve leverage and short-term speculation on whether or not an investment will go up or down within a certain time period; and as with margin there is the possibility you could lose all of your investment or more than you invested. There are definitely documents you do not want to sign without a complete understanding of why you are being asked to sign them and how do the strategies that necessitate their signing fit your investment objectives and risk tolerance.

Do not sign anything that is not completely and properly filled out, or that you do not understand why you are being asked to sign it.

Discretionary Authorization Form

As previously discussed, most people use a broker because they do not want to make investment decisions themselves. They expect the broker to tell them what and when to buy, what and when to sell, and what to do in between. The overwhelming majority of clients say that when their broker calls them with a recommendation they respond with, "Well, if you think that's what we should do, then do it." They even say that they tell the broker not to bother calling them, just do what they think is right. This is sometimes called de facto discretion, where the authorization is understood and unwritten, and something both the client and the broker may want.

The problem for the broker is that there are rules regarding the need to contact a customer before entering an order. Unless the broker has **written** authorization to the contrary, they have to contact their customer first. Accounts without that written authorization are called non-discretionary accounts. That means brokers do not have discretion to enter orders for their clients without prior/contemporaneous permission.

If you want your broker to enter orders for you without contacting you first, and your broker's firm allows that, then this is called a discretionary account. In a discretionary account you give the broker discretion to make trades in your account without asking you first. This discretion must be in writing and usually takes on the form of a limited power of attorney.

One of the reasons some brokerage firms do not allow their brokers to have discretionary authority is that with discretionary authority comes added duties and obligations to the broker and his firm. Brokers with written discretionary authority owe their client a *fiduciary* duty. That is, they have a duty to put their client's interest above their own or their firm's. Even though you would think they should have that duty as a matter of course, the law is only clear that duty exists when a fiduciary duty is established. Otherwise, as in the case of de facto discretion, there is significant wiggle room for brokers when their motives and the suitability of their recommendations are called into question.

So remember, if you want your broker to call the shots and be held more accountable, have the relationship reduced to writing. Otherwise, you may unintentionally be giving your broker a free pass when it comes to accountability.

Confirmations and Statements

Your broker is required to provide you with written confirmation of every transaction that takes place in your account. Each firm's confirmation may look different, but they all will have certain common characteristics. They will have the name of the security, whether it is a buy or a sell, the date of the trade, the date the trade will settle (with a buy order that is the day money is due from you to pay for the trade; with a sell order that is the day money will post to your account), the commission or mark up, and if applicable whether or not the brokerage firm acted as agent or principal in the transaction and/or whether or not they are a market maker in the security. Additionally, there should be an indication as to whether the trade was solicited by the broker, meaning the trade was his idea, or unsolicited, meaning the trade was your idea.

In most cases your broker's firm is also required to send you monthly statements. If there is little to no activity for periods of time, the statements may come quarterly. These statements are as varied as the firms themselves in terms of appearance; however, like confirmations there is certain information common to all. The statement should have your name, address, account number, and your broker's identity. It should recap all of the transactions, deposits, withdrawals, interest charged, interest earned, dividends paid, and any debit balance since the last statement. It should provide you with an account value for all priced securities (some securities, such as limited partnerships, cannot be marked to the market or priced). Most will tell you what you paid for the security, what it is worth as of the statement date, and what your unrealized gain or loss is. Some will tell you what the annual yield is on each security.

Many statements have graphs or pie charts showing the asset allocation in your account; i.e., how much money you have invested in different asset classes like stocks, bonds, mutual funds, and cash.

Many clients say that they never open their "confirms" and if they do open their statements they do not look past the first page where it tells them what their account is worth. Some say this is because their broker has instructed them not to bother. Others say they wouldn't understand it. Still others have said, especially when the market has been going down, that they are afraid to see how they are doing.

It is very important that you open, look at, and save all of your statements and confirmations. You need to be current and understand what is going on in your account at all times, and these are the documents that will assist you in that process. Also, if you find yourself in litigation with your broker it never looks good to the trier of fact that you have not opened or have just thrown away these documents, regardless of the reason. To them, that looks like you do not care about your account; and if you don't care, why should they care about ordering the broker or his firm to give you back some or all of your money?

"Happiness" Letters

What in the business is referred to as "happiness letters" are letters from your broker's firm where they attempt to gloss over some potentially troubling activity with disarming verbiage. For example, their may be a high volume of trading going on in your account resulting in large commissions. Instead of using language alerting you to this fact, they may couch the activity in the form of a "thank you for all of the business you are doing," and to "please call if there is anything you need." As a general rule, if you receive a letter from your broker's firm for no apparent reason, call the person who sent it, usually a compliance person or the branch manager, and ask why the letter was sent. Do not call your broker and ask him what the letter is about. The letter usually has to do with something the broker has done wrong and he knows this, so they may try to dissuade you from following up, or worse, will lie and tell you the letter means nothing. Remember, follow up immediately with the sender and take copious notes of your conversation.

The importance of documents cannot be stressed enough in opening and maintaining a brokerage account. It is your responsibility to make sure that you have read and understood anything you are asked to sign and/or respond to. If you have questions, ask. If you don't understand something, keep asking until you do. If you cannot understand the document, then whatever it is for is probably not for you.

As stated at the beginning of this chapter, the documents associated with opening and maintaining your brokerage account form the cornerstone of the regulatory and compliance structure that brokers and brokerage firms are bound by. It is incumbent upon you as well as the broker to make sure that the information contained in them is accurate, complete, and up to date.

Life-changing events like death, divorce, retirement, unemployment, marriage, the birth of a child, or the selling or buying of a home could have a dramatic impact on your investment objectives and risk tolerance. You need to report them to your broker and make sure they are reflected in your documents. Too many times clients say, "Well, the broker knew about my divorce/retirement/ husband's passing, etc., because I told him," but that information is not reflected or updated in the documents. This makes it difficult for your account activity to be properly supervised and again leaves things in a "he said/he said" state if questions arise later.

CHAPTER 6
HOW CAN I AVOID PROBLEMS?

As with any relationship, especially ones involving money, there is the potential for problems. While you cannot avoid all problems, there are steps you can take along the way to either lessen the opportunity for problems or see to it that problems are resolved in your favor.

Things You Say That Come Back to Haunt You

Regarding the former, here is a list of things that customers say to their broker that come back to haunt them. This list comes from more than twenty-five years in and around the industry as a broker, marketing manager, sales manager, compliance officer and attorney. But it is not exhaustive.

1. "I don't mind signing the forms in blank and having you fill them in later."

2. "I just want to make money."

3. "I'm getting all this stuff in the mail from you; can I just throw it away?"

4. "I don't care; do whatever you want."

5. "What are you telling your other clients?"

6. "I trust you completely."

7. "My husband/wife handles all my money; just talk to him/her."

8. "I don't have time to deal with this stuff; that's what I pay you for."

9. "I understand." (When you don't)

10. "I don't understand, but go ahead."

What most of these have in common is an apparent disregard for what happens to your money. While it is understood that you have decided to use a broker because you feel you cannot manage your funds on your own, never forget that at the end of the day it is your money and no one will or should care more about what happens to it than you.

Further, as much as the brokerage industry spends millions of dollars trying to get you to believe that you need them because the world of investments is too complicated to go it on your own, the great majority of people only need simple, uncomplicated investments, investment advice, and management. Don't stop asking questions until you really do understand what is being said to you. Don't be afraid to appear dumb or unsophisticated. This is your money and you need to understand what is happening with it. If you do not understand what your broker is telling you, it is probably because the product or service is too complicated for your needs.

Things That Brokers Say That Come Back to Haunt Them

Now, here is a list of things that brokers tell their clients that come back to haunt them. As with the previous list, this list comes from my experience in and around the industry, and is not exhaustive.

1. "You don't need to read that; just sign it."
2. "Just write down anything; it doesn't matter."
3. "It won't cost you anything; the issuer/company pays me."
4. "Don't read that; it's just legal stuff."
5. "Don't read that; just throw it away."
6. "I'm buying this for all my clients."
7. "I've put my mother/father/whole family in this."
8. "It works just like a CD."
9. "You can't lose; I guarantee it."
10. "I'm not supposed to tell you this, but…" or, "I have a source inside the company and they told me…"

11. "I'll cover your losses."

12. "Just make the check out to me and I'll take care of it."

13. "I prefer not to put anything in writing; I'll call you."

14. "You can't sell now; it has nowhere to go but up."

15. "Let's just settle this between us; no need to involve anyone else."

Most of these seem obviously wrong for the broker to say, but they are heard over and over again from clients. A broker should never advise you not to read something you are going to sign or that explains something about your account or the investments in it. And just because a broker is putting others into a particular investment, family or not, does not necessarily make it suitable for you.

If your broker says that something he is recommending works just like something else that you may be more familiar and comfortable with, then ask him how is it different and why shouldn't you just buy what you know.

The only investments that are guaranteed not to lose are government issued, and that is only if you hold them to maturity. That is because they have the key to the money printing machine; no one else does. Other "guarantees" are only as good and sound as the people making the guarantee.

Brokers cannot pass on or act on information not available to the general public, cover your losses, or accept funds not made out to either the issuer of the product or the company that handles the money for his firm.

The bottom line is: if it doesn't sound right or sounds too good to be true, then it probably isn't right or it is too good to be true.

Note-taking and Correspondence

The best cases, which by definition means getting the best result either through settlement or an award from an arbitration panel, are not necessarily those with the most sympathetic clients or the most egregious conduct on the part of brokers and/or their firms. They are the cases where the best non-verbal evidence such as notes and correspondence exist.

You should always have a pen and paper handy whenever you speak with your broker, whether it is in his office or on the phone. You do not have to be a court stenographer and take down every word, but you should write down the important issues raised and discussed. Make sure to indicate the date and time of the call/conference, and indicate anyone else that was in attendance. You may even record your phone conversations. In certain states it is legal to tape your phone conversations without informing the other party; be sure to know the law in your state before doing this.

If email is your preferred method of communication, make sure you get an emailed response back. Brokers' emails are monitored and for that reason many of them do not like to commit to writing something they would not want coming back to them later. But it is precisely for that reason that you want to make sure there is a written memorial of what you said and what your broker said. The less that is left to memory, the better you are. If your broker is not willing to let you take notes, or to put his ideas, recommendations, etc., into written words, that should be a real red flag for you.

You cannot always avoid problems, but if you follow the advice in this chapter the chances that the problems will be resolved in your favor are greatly enhanced.

CHAPTER 7
DEALING WITH PROBLEMS

Okay, you have done everything you were supposed to do but your broker and/or his firm Did not, and because of that you have lost money. What can you do?

Put it in Writing

First, put your complaint in writing and send it to your broker's supervisor. If your complaint is with the supervisor, send your complaint to the firm's home office to the attention of their compliance department and/or their general counsel. Be clear, concise, and include as much supporting documentation as possible. Say that you want the matter resolved and give them a reasonable time frame to respond; I would suggest anywhere from two weeks to a month, depending on how complicated the issues are and how much research they will have to perform.

Do not expect a favorable response. The real purpose is not getting the matter resolved, but rather to start a paper trail for the trier of fact. You want to show from the outset that you tried to resolve this matter without resorting to litigation, but you were summarily denied or ignored by the offending party. You always want to be perceived as being the good person throughout this process.

Also, by putting your complaint in writing, it becomes part of the broker's permanent record. He and his firm have to report all complaints to the regulators, and some brokers and firms have been known to come down with temporary amnesia in this regard when there is no written evidence of the complaint.

Arbitration

So, what next? The answer is found in every customer agreement at every brokerage firm in this country. It says, in some form or fashion: if you have a complaint and you want to sue, you cannot go to court but instead you have to submit to binding arbitration.

Arbitration is a form of alternative dispute resolution, away from the courthouse. The origins, statutes, and case law that resulted in this being the legal and accepted forum for hearing disputes of this nature are not important for the purposes of this book. Suffice it to say that arbitration is a court or forum of equity, versus a court or forum of law. The arbitrators are the triers of fact and it is their charge and duty to administer and dispense justice in accordance with the rules of the forum and as their interpretation of the facts and evidence presented to them so dictates. Their decision is binding, with very limited grounds for appeal.

The agreement will go on to say that you must submit to arbitration pursuant to the rules of the Financial Industry Regulatory Authority (FINRA). FINRA is the self-regulatory organization charged with oversight of brokers and brokerage firms. It is comprised of and funded in part by the membership dues of the brokers and firms they are charged with overseeing.

Do I Have a Good Case?

This is the question on the mind of everyone who has lost money and is considering going the next step: submitting to arbitration. Losing money in and of itself is not a cause of action. If that were the case, the arbitration system would be flooded on a perpetual basis, as not a day goes by that someone does not lose money in their investments. You have to be able to match the loss with some action or inaction on the part of the broker and/or the broker's firm in order to have a chance at recovering some or all of your losses.

If you decide to contact an attorney to represent you, and this attorney has experience in handling securities arbitration, this is the likely analysis that they will go through. This analysis will also be helpful to you if you decide to represent yourself in determining whether or not you should invest the time, emotional and financial capital, and effort needed to bring a claim.

They start their assessment the minute you call and they hear your voice for the first time. How do you sound? How do you present yourself and your situation? Are you articulate or incoherent? Do you sound sincere? Why is any of this important? These issues will all be incredibly important in determining whether or not a case has merit and value. The reason is arbitration is a court of equity, not a court of law. While we would like to think that if we present strong, cogent legal arguments supported by common law and/or statute, the law will carry the day. The reality is that arbitration is for the most part "arbitrary," and while there are as many theories as cases as to why arbitrators do what they do, the one constant is if the arbitrators do not *like* you or feel sympathy for you on some level, the arbitrators are very unlikely to award you any money. While an attorney can prep you in anticipation of your testimony, when you get on the witness stand, you will be who you are, and that is what the arbitrators will see and hear. Usually those first few interactions on the phone or in person with you will give the attorney a good feeling about whether or not you are someone the arbitrators will want to award money.

With that backdrop, attorneys listen to potential clients in a certain way. Specifically, they will listen for two things: a hook and a link. The hook is that bad act or acts that set your case apart from, "I lost money, so somebody must have done something wrong." Sometimes that is easy, or easier, as in cases where a broker makes an investment or a trade that you did not authorize, or in the case where your investment objective was "income" and the broker did not recommend any income-producing investments.

Other times, as in most cases where suitability is at issue, the hook may be more difficult. What you should always keep in mind, especially in times when the overall market has suffered a decline, is that you must be able to differentiate your situation from that of the arbitrator's. What I mean is that most if not all of the arbitrators are sophisticated businesspeople, who for the most part are investors themselves in the securities markets in one form or another. Their mind-set is, "I lost money, too, and no one is giving me my money back; so why should I award you money that is unavailable to me as an investor?"

You need to be able to articulate and demonstrate what circumstances make you deserving of an award. Are you elderly? Are you retired and attempting to live modestly? Are you infirm? Are you uneducated or under-educated, both from a scholastic and investment standpoint? These are the types of people that are most unlike the arbitrators, who are often working, successful, and educated both scholastically and financially, and who thus stand a better chance of recovering lost money.

In addition, it is important that you can answer five questions: Who filled out the new account worksheet/forms? When or did you receive a copy of it? Did you open your confirmations and monthly statements when you received them? When did you first discover something was wrong? What did you do at that point?

New Account Forms are important, as this is in many instances the one document that purports to lay out your investment objective(s) and risk tolerance. In many instances the broker took down the information over the phone, or a sales assistant took down the information, or you were just asked to sign a blank form that the broker told you would be filled in later. Remember from a previous chapter, this is the document that theoretically controls what investment recommendations are suitable for the broker to make, and the document that the broker's supervisor is to refer to when reviewing trades for suitability. As a result, your understanding of, participation in, and review of the information found on these documents is crucial to your case.

The question concerning whether you received and read the confirmations and monthly statements go to the "M" word, *mitigation*. Mitigate means to make less severe. While in theory, and even according to some statutes, you may not have a legal duty to mitigate damages, the reality is most arbitration panel members want to know and will most likely consider what you did to protect yourself from harm. If you have a banker's box of three years worth of unopened confirms and statements, a possible indication that you were not keeping track of what was going on in your account, is not a good thing. Arbitrators expect you on some level to take an interest in your life savings, which in many cases is what is at stake.

The, "I trusted my broker," or "my broker told me not to look at those things," or "I wouldn't understand what they said anyway" explanations are reasonable and acceptable…to a point. Rightly or wrongly, at some point in the broker/client relationship, especially where the bad conduct takes place over a number of years, the arbitrators will start to shift some of the blame and accountability for what happened to you. You need to be able to exhibit a reasonable level of due diligence in your own affairs, which in this case means at least opening statements and confirmations when you received them, in order to show the arbitrators that you were holding up your end of the bargain.

The second thing the attorney will be listening for in your initial conversation is the link. The link is being able to tie the conduct complained of to your damages. While in most cases that is not too difficult, i.e., unsuitable recommendation leads to losses, there are instances when making that connection is tricky. Cases that depend to a great degree on lack of supervision, and/or where there is an empty chair (broker is in prison for selling fraudulent investments or outright theft, or the broker is deceased), and violations of internal policies are examples of more complex cases. Most arbitrators like nice, neat simple cases. When it comes to liability, they want you to give them the financial equivalent of the robber standing over the body with the gun in their hand, the smoke still coming from the barrel and no one else in sight. Keep in mind as a general rule, the more removed the claim is from the person who did you wrong, the more work must be done to convince the panel to award you damages.

If during your initial meetings and/or conversations with the attorney, you find both a hook and a link, and the attorney believes you will be likeable, and you can distinguish your losses from the kinds of losses the arbitrators may have also suffered (making it more likely they will award you money), then the documents you have to support your position will come into play. These should include the New Account Form, New Account Worksheets, copies of statements and confirmations (if they are unopened, leave them that way), any correspondence in any form, i.e. letters, emails, faxes, and any charts, graphs, and hypothetical illustrations you were shown. If you have taped any conversations between you and the broker or his firm, the attorney will want to hear those as well. (Reminder: if you are going to tape conversations, make sure you know the law in your state regarding whether or not you need to tell the other party you are taping the conversation.)

What you and the attorney will be looking for are consistencies or inconsistencies between what you say happened and what the documents say happened. One of the key items your attorney will look for is withdrawals from the account. Sometimes people remember how much they started with and how much they have now and "forget" that they took out money. There may be justification for the withdrawals, but you need to be understand there may be a difference in how much the account lost versus the difference between starting and ending balances, which may include significant withdrawals. This is important because arbitrators do not typically consider withdrawals as losses, in that withdrawals are money you spent and received some benefit from the use of that money.

So if you started the account with five-hundred thousand dollars and three years later have a balance of two-hundred-fifty thousand dollars, but during that three years have withdrawn two-hundred thousand dollars for living expenses, travel, loans to family members, etc., then arbitrators will most likely consider your losses to be fifty thousand dollars, not two-hundred-fifty thousand.

If there is a significant amount of activity in a number of securities in several accounts that spans several years, you may want to consider having a damage analysis done up front instead of waiting until later in the process. What this means is that you may want the accounts looked at by someone who specializes in reviewing securities account statements and confirmations and preparing damage reports to determine what your actual losses are.

You can have the losses broken down any number of ways. For example, they can be broken down by types of securities. This is important when overconcentration or lack of diversification is an issue. Many times the broker tells the client that they are diversified because they own several different funds, but a closer analysis reveals that the holdings of the different funds are quite similar.

They can break them down by trading costs including commissions, fees, and margin interest. This is important when the account is being traded again and again, otherwise known as churning.

Additionally, most of these people can also prepare what is referred to as an "alternative damage model" or "well-managed portfolio." What this will show is what the value of your account would have been if your portfolio had been properly or suitably invested. Sometimes this number is more than your actual losses, sometimes less. The purpose is two-fold: (1) to put into dollars the difference between what the broker did and what the broker should have done, and (2) in the event the model number is higher, to give the arbitrators a basis to give you more than your actual losses.

The important thing is that you have a feel for the value of the case so you can discuss it at the outset and set your expectation level for recovery accordingly. Having a realistic view of the case and expectations is crucial from the outset. Nothing is worse than battling the other side and your own side at the same time. You need to know the strengths and weaknesses of your case, not only from a fact specific perspective but relative to the forum, arbitration through FINRA. You need to know what is reasonable to expect, which may differ significantly from what is fair and just.

Describing Arbitration

How can arbitration through FINRA be described? Here is an example: Imagine you are mugged by a member of a large gang. He takes some if not all of your life savings. You want justice and the return of your money, so you go to court. The court says, "No, you cannot come here. We have a different place for you to go to seek justice."

They tell you the place you will be going, as luck would have it, is run by the gang of which your mugger is a dues-paying member in good standing. The leaders of the gang have established the rules under which you will be able to seek justice. They have determined who is and who is not qualified to be considered as someone who is able to pass judgment. The people representing the gang member who mugged you are rarely if ever punished for not playing by the rules that the gang leadership set up, and among the rules the gang leadership established is a rule that one third of the people who will decide your case are either gang members or affiliated with the gang.

So why would anybody subject themselves to this? Because – if you want any chance of recovering your losses, this is the *only* option.

On the bright side, the arbitration process through FINRA is on the whole cheaper, faster, and less caught up in legal procedure than court. The rules discourage taking depositions or, serving and answering long lists of questions, known as interrogatories. You also do not have to be familiar with the rules of civil procedure or evidence, as they do not apply. There is a FINRA Code of Arbitration Procedure (CAP) that you must follow, but it is written in plain English as opposed to legalese.

Additionally, there is no set format to pleading your case. The rules dictate that the complaint, otherwise known as the Statement of Claim, need only contain sufficient information as to apprise the other side of what it is you are complaining about and what you want as a remedy. You do not need to tie the conduct to a specific law or rule violation. Further, there is no specific form or format you need to follow in drafting your Statement of Claim, you can just write it out as if you were telling it to a friend in a letter.

Costs

There are five major costs you need to consider in deciding to file a claim; four of them are monetary and one is non-monetary. The four monetary costs are:

1. Filing Fee
2. Attorneys Fees
3. Expert Witness Fees
4. Forum Fees

Filing Fee

The filing fee is the fee FINRA assesses for you to bring the claim and for them to administer it. The fee is on a sliding scale based on the amount of damages you are claiming. For example, as of the fee adjustments in April 2007 for cases with claimed damages between five- and ten-thousand dollars, the fee is $325.00. If the claim is between fifty- and one-hundred thousand dollars, the fee is $975.00. If the claim is between one-hundred and five-hundred-thousand dollars, the fee is $1,425.00, and if it is over a million dollars, the fee tops out at $1,800.00.

Attorneys' Fees

Should you decide to hire an attorney to represent you (a discussion of this follows below), most experienced securities arbitration attorneys handle these types of cases on a contingency fee basis. That is their fees are a percentage of any money you collect through award or settlement. If you do not collect, they do not get paid. The contingency fee is typically between twenty-five and forty percent, depending upon the facts, competition in the area, and the attorney's reputation and applicable state law with regard to contingency fees. You may ask that the arbitrators award you your attorneys' fees as part of your damages, but having them actually do that is the exception not the rule.

Expert Witness Fees

In many cases it is advisable or even necessary to retain the services of one or more experts. These are people, usually with industry or regulatory experience, who provide advice/opinions/testimony to you, your attorney, and the arbitrators. They typically work for either a flat fee or on an hourly rate basis. Depending upon what is needed to support your particular case you can expect to pay anywhere from twenty-five hundred to twenty-five thousand dollars in expert witness fees from start to finish. As with attorneys' fees, you may ask that the arbitrators award you your expert witness fees as part of your damages, but having them actually do that is the exception not the rule.

Forum Fees

The forum fees are the fees that FINRA assesses throughout the course of the proceedings for the arbitrators' time. Each time one or more arbitrators are engaged in dealing with your matter, they track and turn in their time to FINRA. At the end of the matter, either through settlement or through the hearing, FINRA totals up the time and sends each side a bill for their share. The arbitrators have discretion on how to apportion the forum fees between the parties, and FINRA has the ability to waive some or all of these fees based on circumstances and need at their discretion. The majority of these fees come from the arbitrators attending the hearing itself, so if the matter is settled before a hearing or the hearing is short the forum fees will be far less than if there is a protracted hearing over many days and/or weeks.

Non-monetary Cost

The fifth and non-monetary cost associated with this process is the cost the entire experience takes on you and your family emotionally, regardless of whether or not you hire an attorney to represent you. This is a cost you should not overlook or underestimate. While arbitration is not a court of law, it is still court. The time and energy you will spend looking for documents and reliving and retelling the events over and over is taxing and draining, not to mention the stress associated with testifying at the hearing if your case does not settle.

Your attorney may play devil's advocate with you and may even have you go through a mock cross examination, but it cannot and will not compare to what an actual cross examination by an experienced defense counsel is like. In most instances defense attorneys are given wide latitude in how they cross-examine their witnesses, and arbitrators want to hear the whole story without a lot of objections from the attorneys. Most people have never experienced cross-examination, where you are not allowed to argue with the person posing the questions, ask your own questions, or decide which questions you want to answer and which ones you don't.

The stress, anger, and anxiety clients experience on the witness stand is unlike anything else they have ever experienced, including divorce, losing a job, or losing a loved one.

Do I Need an Attorney?

So, do you need an attorney to pursue your case? The answer is: you don't *need* an attorney but, as we say in the profession when an attorney chooses to represent themselves in litigation, "The attorney who represents himself has a fool for a client."

If you choose to go it alone, or *pro se*, you must understand that the brokerage firms will have lawyers proficient in this process, either in-house or in the form of outside counsel. Many of the lawyers I face do nothing but defend brokers and brokerage firms. They know the rules and, more importantly, how to use or bend them to their advantage. While many arbitrators may cut a pro se a little slack at first, in the end you will be held to the same standard of knowing and obeying the CAP, just as if you were being represented by counsel.

Some of the biggest awards and easiest hearings have been against brokers who chose to represent themselves. The same is said to be true from the other side. Defense counsel usually say that their easiest cases are the ones where the claimant is *pro se*. There simply is no substitute for experience.

Arbitrator Selection

If you chose to be *pro se,* you will be at a decided disadvantage in one of the most critical aspects of securities arbitration, ranking/selecting the arbitrators that will decide your fate. If your claim is over fifty thousand dollars, the CAP calls for a panel of three arbitrators. Two will be classified as "non-industry" or "public," and the third will be employed by, recently retired from, or associated with the brokerage industry. One of the two public arbitrators will serve as the chairperson of the panel. The chair's vote does not count any more than the other arbitrator's; it is his/her job as chair to lead pre-hearing conferences, resolve discovery disputes, rule on objections at the hearing, and generally keep the process moving in an orderly fashion.

Each side receives from FINRA three lists of potential arbitrators: one list for chairperson, one list for public non-chairperson, and one list for industry. There are eight names on each list. The names are drawn from the pool of arbitrators closest to where the hearing will be held (typically this is the city closest to where the bad acts took place and where FINRA has designated as a hearing city). The pool of arbitrators is made up of individuals who have applied to FINRA to serve as arbitrators, filled out an extensive application, which includes three letters of recommendation, paid a fee, and attended a training class. These people are not employees of FINRA, but many of them have current or past ties to the industry, and in most cases are far more sophisticated and less likely to empathize with clients in terms of experience or sophistication.

With the three lists you will receive what is called an Arbitrator Disclosure Report for each potential arbitrator. The report will give the arbitrator's name, classification, employment history, education history, training, conflict disclosures, a narrative from the arbitrator on his background, and a list of publically available awards if the person has been an arbitrator in the past.

You may strike up to four names from each list for any reason. Then you must rank in order of preference the names you do not strike. You will not have an opportunity to meet or speak with these people before making your selections. You are allowed to send them a list of questions, but they do not have to respond, and in my experience do not respond.

Their prior award history is somewhat helpful in that you can get a sense for how frequently and how much they have awarded to people filing claims in the past. But the awards are not reasoned, meaning the arbitrators do not have to explain what went on during the hearing or how they reached their conclusion, so it is hard to gauge how they might respond to your particular set of facts.

That is where an experienced securities arbitration lawyer comes in. If they have done enough of these types of cases they will have a knowledge base of who the good arbitrators are and who to avoid. If they don't have first-hand knowledge, they should have access to other attorneys that practice in this field to assist them in optimally ranking and striking. *There is no set of facts, no matter how egregious, that can make up for a bad arbitrator.* Anything you can do that will give you an edge in the selection process is worth doing, and that usually means hiring an experienced securities arbitration attorney.

Discovery

The discovery process, while less costly and time consuming because of the lack of depositions and interrogatories as previously mentioned, is none the less very intrusive and frustrating. You will be expected to voluntarily turn over documents that appear to have nothing to do with your claim, such as tax returns, other investment account information, and financial records, unless you can show good cause as to why these are not relevant.

On the other hand, you can expect to receive very little from the other side without a knock-down, drag-out battle. This is because the brokerage firms and their counsel know that they will rarely suffer the types of consequences that a court could and would impose on them for their lack of cooperation. However, more will be expected of you since you are bringing the claim; the burden of proof rests with you and the CAP requires it. If this sounds inequitable, that is because it is.

Settlement Negotiations

At some point in the process one side or the other will broach the subject of settlement. This should not be taken as a sign of weakness, regardless of who brings it up. Most securities arbitrations, like most litigation in general, results in the parties agreeing to a settlement rather than rolling the dice in a trial/hearing, where there are too any unknowns that could affect the outcome.

How to negotiate a settlement is a book in itself, but here are some facts you need to know, because the other side knows them and will use them. You need to know that in the first decade of the new century – the win rate for claimants that chose to go through an arbitration hearing rather than settle declined from a high of fifty-nine to sixty percent to as low as thirty-seven percent. That means that claimants walked away with nothing in more six out of ten cases that went to hearing. This is not anecdotal information; these published statistics can be found on FINRA's website www. finra.org.

Bear in mind that according to FINRA a win is any case where the claimant is awarded any money. So if your claim was for a million dollars and a panel awarded you five-thousand dollars, FINRA counts that as a win for claimants, even though after taking into account all the fees and expenses, the claimant may actually have lost money in bringing the claim. Additionally, there have been studies done that show the win rate for claimants is even lower when their claims are against the big brokerage firms like Merrill Lynch and UBS PaineWebber. What this means is that brokerage firms, large and small, know their chances of losing and losing big in a case that does not settle and goes all the way to hearing are relatively small.

They also know that the likelihood you will be awarded costs, attorneys' fees, interest, and punitive damages are very small. This is the case even if the legal basis under which you are asserting your claims calls for or allows attorneys' fees, costs, and interest to be awarded.

You need to know all this in order to evaluate any settlement offers that may come up. When discussing settlement with clients they always ask what a fair amount to settle for would be. Fair has nothing to do with it. Fair would be all their money back, plus all fees costs and interest, plus lost opportunity costs, plus something for all their trouble. To evaluate settlement offers is to ask what is the offer compared to what a panel might award when faced with the facts and circumstances. This is based on knowledge of the panel and what experience dictates. It is not an exact science.

If the settlement negotiations take place in mediation, then I am interested in the mediator's perspective, provided he is an experienced securities mediator who has also served as an arbitrator. Mediation is a method of dispute resolution where the parties retain the services of a trained neutral third party who assists each side in evaluating their respective strengths and weaknesses and tries to help them reach a mutually agreeable, or disagreeable as the case may be, resolution to their issues. The mediator has no stake in the outcome and is not a decision maker. The process is voluntary and non-binding unless the parties reach an agreement; then the agreement becomes binding and the case is over.

The Hearing

If you do not resolve your case through settlement negotiations, then prepare for the hearing. A securities arbitration hearing is unlike any other form or forum of dispute resolution. Many an experienced trial lawyer will throw up their hands in dismay/disgust/ and outright disbelief when they experience securities arbitration first hand.

As stated, you are truly walking into the lion's den. This is the industry's forum and rules. While FINRA holds itself out as an investor protection agency, and certainly makes efforts in support of that position, the statistics on the win rate for investors in FINRA arbitration do not lie. For 2007 (www.finra.org, accessed Dec. '09) more than six out every ten people who went to hearing walked away with nothing, or possibly less than nothing if they are assessed forum fees and/or have costs they are responsible for paying.

There are no rules of evidence or procedure, save the CAP, and its interpretation is left up to each individual chairperson and panel as they see fit. There is no reliance on prior decisions of other panels; each panel makes up its own mind based on the testimony and evidence presented in each particular case. Other than persons directly involved in the case, i.e. you, your broker, his supervisor/ control person at the firm, and each side's respective expert witnesses, no one else will testify or be in the hearing room (except your spouse, if you wish). You can't bring a friend for moral support or to testify on your behalf. Panels do not award pain and suffering damages, so you will not be allowed to put on medical testimony of how this loss has affected your health and sanity.

For the most part panels want to hear your story and the broker/ brokerage firm's story in its entirety and with little interruption from counsel. They may or may not be interested in what your respective experts have to say, but they know that each side is paying their expert and presumably would not have hired someone that did not see the facts their way.

Expert Witnesses

That brings up the question frequently by clients, "Do I need an expert?" Experts are like nuclear weapons, when each side has one they tend to cancel each other out but when only one side has one the other side is in danger. And rest assured, the brokerage firms will come with an expert.

The single most frustrating part of arbitration is that the panels do not have to, and typically do not, give you reasons for their awards. Typically, you ask for an amount of damages commensurate with the harm you believe was done unto you and the brokerage firm will ask that you be awarded nothing. The panel can award you everything you ask for, nothing, or anything in between. They do not have to tell you or anyone why or how they reached their decision. They are not bound by law or statute, only their individual and collective conscience as to what is fair and equitable. Each arbitrator brings to a hearing his own sense of what is right and what is wrong, what is reasonable and what is unreasonable.

There are very few recognizable reasons for a court to vacate an arbitration award. It is the ultimate power trip to decide someone's fate with little to no chance of being questioned or overruled.

This highlights one of the few bright spots in the process. If you do win, and collectability is not an issue because the entity you brought your claim against is financially viable, you should get paid. The CAP states the arbitrators are to render their decision within twenty days from the close of the hearing. If there is an award in your favor the broker or brokerage firm has thirty days to pay or be subject to suspension. That means not allowed to do business – *at all*. Nothing gets a broker or his firm's attention faster than a call from FINRA on the 31st day after an award is issued telling them that if they do not pay immediately they are out of business until they pay up, especially if it is a large, well-known firm.

Like swine flu, arbitration hearings are something to be avoided if at all possible. But if you have the financial equivalent of swine flu symptoms, i.e. broker misconduct, followed by non-response leading to a loss of money, then you may have no choice but to deal with the bug. If that is the case, prepare yourself to the best of your ability and bring in specialists to help you deal with the virus.

CHAPTER 8
PONZI SCHEMES

A Ponzi scheme is a fraudulent investment operation where promised returns are actually made from the investor's investment dollars or from money paid by subsequent investors, but not from any
actual investment. The scheme is named after Charles Ponzi, who
used this technique in the early 1920s with regard to trading or
arbitraging international reply coupons for postage stamps.

There are two key elements to a successful Ponzi scheme: a breakdown in oversight or supervision, and promised returns that are
irresistible to the investor. These elements also serve as the red
flags that should alert you to the possibility of being caught up in
a Ponzi scheme. These are the same elements and red flags that
were present in two prominent Ponzi schemes in 2008-09: the
Bernard Madoff and Allen Stanford scandals.

The scheme will typically involve a product or a complex, sophisticated investment strategy that offers/promises high, consistent re-

turns that cannot be achieved through anyone else but that broker/firm. High, consistent returns are key, because for a scheme to work for an extended period of time investors cannot want to take out their money and new money must keep coming in. If the returns are high and consistent, why would you want to take your money out, and why wouldn't you put more money in as it became available as well as recommend the investment to others?

In the case of the Madoff scheme, he was promising and delivering consistent, month-in month-out, year-in year-out returns to his investors using a complex, option based strategy that, according to Madoff, only he could understand and execute. He was doing this regardless of underlying market conditions and economics. Whether it was the doldrums of the early nineties, the international debt crisis of the late nineties or the technology meltdown of the early part of this century, Madoff managed to deliver consistent, positive returns when virtually no one else could.

In hindsight you would have thought that his select clientele, many of them sophisticated high net worth individuals and institutions, would have questioned Madoff's success; but instead they took the "head in the sand" position. On some level that is understandable. However, those charged with the oversight and supervision of Madoff's brokerage operation apparently took the same "head in the sand" position, and that is what allowed the Ponzi scheme to be successful and continue for approximately twenty years.

In the case of Stanford, he was promising and delivering higher than normal returns on certificates of deposit, issued offshore. As with Madoff, he was dealing for the most part with a high net worth and sophisticated clientele that should have had suspicions about how Stanford was able to deliver returns that no one else could. And, as with Madoff, proper supervision and oversight on the part of those charged with that responsibility would in all likelihood have detected and put an end to the scheme before so much financial devastation was done.

In both cases, Madoff and Stanford, what brought them down was what brings down most Ponzi schemes: lack of liquidity. That is, new money has to keep coming in to pay the old investors their returns, while at the same time no one previously invested can take out their principal. If new money does not come in and/or people need or want to start taking out principal instead of just being happy with a return on their investment, the scheme will unravel.

While Madoff and Stanford are examples of what can happen to supposedly sophisticated clients dealing with non-traditional brokers/firms, the same schemes take place at more traditional brokerage firms, regardless of size, every day.

A breakdown in oversight or supervision can be more prevalent in the small to mid-size brokerage firms. These are firms like Edward Jones, Ameriprise, Raymond James, and LPL, to name a few, whose business model is to have one or two brokers in a branch office, with no on-site supervisor or compliance officer. Supervision and compliance are centrally located somewhere else and usually delegated by region.

The brokers at these firms have a policies, procedures, and compliance manuals to follow, and are subject to both internal audits as well as audits conducted by regulators, but on a day-to-day basis they are left to their own devices as to whether or not they will play by the rules. Brokers in these firms will typically handle client funds when a client comes in, as there is no on-site cashier. They will also handle their own mail, which includes the receipt of client funds.

The larger firms like Merrill Lynch/Bank of America, UBS, Wachovia/Wells Fargo, and Morgan Stanley Smith Barney, where there are many brokers and staff in each branch office, will usually have an on-site branch manager, administrative manager, compliance officer, and cashier. Brokers at these firms do not handle client funds or receive mail that has not already been opened.

The autonomy and seemingly more personalized approach provided by the small to mid-size firm model, which many brokers and their clients find appealing, lends itself more readily to the carrying out of Ponzi schemes. The broker/schemer needs to control the inflow and outflow of information and funds, and this is easier to do at the smaller to mid-size firms for the reasons stated above.

Further, in all likelihood the scheme investment will not show up on your monthly statement like your other investments at the firm. The broker's explanation may be that this is a product or strategy that is being offered on the side, away from the firm. That will also account for why the distribution/profit checks you receive will not come from the broker's firm, but from some third party or even the broker themselves.

Or, you may get the explanation that it is an oversight and will show up on the next statement. Each month you will hear some variation on that theme, with the hope that after you start receiving the promised high returns/distributions you will not concern yourself with whether or not the investment is reflected anywhere.

There are also cases where the broker will manufacture and distribute fraudulent statements that may include legitimate investments as well as the schemed investments. This is easier to get away with when the client does not have prior brokerage experience and does not know what to look for in a legitimate statement. If the monthly statement comes from the broker's local office address as opposed to a firm's home office address, or the broker delivers the statement to you in person, that should be a red flag that something is amiss.

The single most important thing to remember and bear in mind to keep you from becoming a victim of a Ponzi scheme is: *If it sounds too good to be true, then it probably is too good to be true.* It does not take an advanced degree in finance or years of market experience to know that if you are being offered something that is better than anything else out there, be it a rate of return on a CD or a bond or an investment strategy that always makes money regardless of market conditions, something is not right.

Do not get caught up in herd mentality; just because many others are doing it does not make it right. Ask questions. Be critical. Ask yourself (and the broker) how can they deliver a product or strategy that no one else can. Ask others with more investment experience if what the broker is telling you makes sense. If you do not know anyone to ask, contact your state securities commission and tell them what is being offered/told to you. While they will probably not give you investment advice, they should tell you whether or not what the broker is saying makes sense or what further questions to ask the broker.

Remember, *if it sounds too good to be true, then it probably is too good to be true.*

CHAPTER 9
SELLING AWAY

Sometimes brokers will offer investments that are not sold through and/or approved by the brokerage firm they are affiliated with. This practice is referred to as "selling away," as the broker is selling away from the products and services offered by the firm.

Brokers may engage in selling away for a number of reasons. One reason is they are working for a smaller firm that does not carry a full range of products like the one the broker wants to sell to you. The firm may not have the due diligence capacity and resources to properly evaluate and/or participate in the product, but the broker wants to sell it nonetheless. This is sometimes the case with insurance-based products that may have a securities component, like a variable annuity, where the broker has a separate insurance license to sell this type of product because the firm does not have an insurance division.

Another reason may be that a special situation has come up and they have an opportunity to earn a fee or commission outside the firm. For example, the broker may have a friend or client that is offering shares in a privately held company, or is putting together a limited partnership to own a building or piece of property, and he is offered a commission or fee to sell shares/units in the investment.

Almost all brokerage firms have internal policies and procedures that deal with the issue of selling away. Some firms don't allow their brokers to sell any investments that are not sold through the firm, under any circumstances. Some firms will allow the practice, but only after the broker has made full disclosure to the firm about the investment and it has been approved by management. In some instances the brokerage firm will require the broker to sign an indemnification agreement so that in the event the brokerage firm is sued for something related to the outside investment the broker agrees to defend the firm and/or pay all costs and damages the firm may incur or be found liable for by a trier of fact.

As the customer/buyer, what you want to know is whether the investment is being offered/sold through the brokerage firm. The best way to determine that is to see if the investment shows up on your monthly statement. If it doesn't, then notwithstanding excuses or protestations to the contrary from the broker, the likelihood is that the firm is not aware of the investment.

Your other option is to call the broker's manager or supervisor and ask if the investment is being sold through the firm. When the broker is operating as a one-person office it may not be easy to discern who the manager is, and you may be hesitant to confront the broker and ask for this information. In that case, go to the firm's website and contact the home office. They should tell you who the supervisor is and/or if the investment is being sold through the firm.

The reason this is important is in the event something goes wrong with the investment. You want to know who should/is going to take responsibility. In selling away cases, brokerage firms take the position that they are not responsible for actions taken by the broker who by their definition is outside of the scope of their employment/affiliation with the firm. They argue that investments the broker sells to clients that are not from the firm's approved list of investments are between the broker and the client and thus are outside the scope of the broker's affiliation with the firm. And since the firm has no knowledge of them and/or not approved them, they should not be held responsible in the event something goes awry.

This position, however, is not necessarily determinative of what their actual responsibility is in the case of selling away. As in the case of Ponzi schemes and as discussed previously, the question comes down to supervision, oversight, and policies and procedures. The question is actually broken into two parts: (1) Does the firm have supervision, oversight, and policies and procedures reasonably designed to cover matters such as selling away? And, (2) Do they have a system to determine if those policies and procedures are actually being followed and implemented?

For example, a firm may say it has a rule against brokers selling investments to clients that are not offered through the firm, but how do they monitor the broker's activities to see if the broker is in compliance with the rule? Do they have regular audits of the broker? Do they monitor his incoming and outgoing correspondence, especially if the broker works from home and has more than one email account? If the broker has a lifestyle that is not supported by the fees and commissions generated from the firm, what are they doing to ascertain where the money is coming from to support that lifestyle? Does the broker have a prior history of selling away? This is not an exhaustive list but are the types of questions a trier of fact will want answers to in deciding whether or not to hold a firm responsible in a selling way case. Obviously, from the client's perspective, the more potential parties that can be liable for the damages suffered in the selling away case, the better.

Remember, as with everything discussed in this book, if you are not sure, ask questions. In the case of selling away, where you are most likely being shown an investment that is outside the traditional stock, bond, or mutual fund that you can follow in the newspaper, make sure you understand who is standing behind the investment and that you have the documentation to support what you are being told.

CONCLUSION

The information in this book may not make you a smarter investor or make you a fortune, but it will hopefully make you a smarter consumer of financial services and help you keep your fortune. Keep in mind a few truisms:

1. Brokers are salespeople. They make money by convincing you to buy and sell. Treat them and view them as you would anyone trying to sell you something: with a healthy dose of skepticism.

2. The money they make, either in commission or fees, is a drag on your investment returns that has to be justified and overcome. If your investment earned four percent in a year, but you paid three percent in commissions and fees, then you only earned one percent.

3. Making money is not synonymous with suitable recommendations, nor is losing money synonymous with
   unsuitable recommendations. Suitability is a determination made at the point of recommendation, not after
   you see how it performed.

4. Absent a fiduciary duty, expect your broker to put their
   interests and those of their firm before your interests.

5. Never sign any document that is blank. Never agree
   to something you do not understand, and never say
   you understand something when you don't. If it can't
   be explained to you so that you can understand it, you
   probably don't need it.

6. Don't throw anything out. Keep a file, shoebox, or
   banker's box of everything you receive from your
   broker and the firm, no matter how tedious or cumbersome this may seem. Open all your correspondence
   and look at it. If you do not understand something, ask.

7. Take notes.

8. If it sounds too good to be true, it probably is.

9. When in doubt, don't sign or agree. Nothing is good
   only at that moment. If you have to act that quickly,
   it's probably not for you.

10. Seek competent counsel at the first sign of trouble.

Remember, not all brokers and investment advisors are bad, just
the ones that are.